THE STORY OF
HORSES

The friendship between man and horse goes back for many centuries, to the very beginning of history. From the first civilizations until the coming of the automobile in the twentieth century, man depended on the horse to carry him from place to place, to transport his goods, to plow his fields, and serve him in hundreds of ways in peace and in war.

In this book, Pat Johnson tells the story of that friendship. She tells of the ancestors of the horse, and of how early man and the horse became partners. She describes how horses were used in ancient warfare, how new breeds were developed for different purposes, and how horses helped to settle America. And finally she tells how horses continue to serve man and bring him pleasure today.

THE STORY OF
HORSES

by **PAT JOHNSON**
Illustrated with photographs by
WALTER D. OSBORNE

Random House
New York

For helpful suggestions about this book, the author and the publisher are grateful to Shirley M. Skinner of the Frick Laboratory, The American Museum of Natural History.

PHOTOGRAPH CREDITS: The American Museum of Natural History, 14, 17, 19, 22, 24-25, 27, 47, 59; British Museum, 35; The Metropolitan Museum of Art, 43, (The Cesnola Collection, 1874-76), 31, (Joseph Pulitzer Bequest, 1942), 38; New York Historical Society, 8, 12, 54-55, 66-67.
All other photographs are by Walter D. Osborne.
Designed by Jackie Mabli.

Contents

THE STORY OF
HORSES

The Horse,
Man's Partner

Most of us usually think of horses as pets—strong, beautiful, friendly animals to play with and ride. Horses can be used in many different ways to give us pleasure. There are swift racers who thunder toward the finish line at the race track. There are powerful jumpers who can leap hurdles higher than a man. There are dazzling beauties who strut and prance around the show ring. We use horses to enjoy many sports, such as riding, polo, hunting, horse show competition and the thrilling events of the rodeo. Today we practically always use horses for some sort of fun and excitement.

If you were going to take a trip from New York to Florida, you would not expect to go by horseback. If you bought a package at a store and wanted it de-

Today we use horses in such sports as riding, racing, and the exciting events of the rodeo.

livered to your home, you would be very surprised if it arrived by horse and wagon. If you wrote a letter to a friend in Boston, you would never dream of its being carried there by horse and rider.

Today we have cars, planes, trucks and trains to transport ourselves and all the things we need. Our fathers do not need a horse to go to the office or to mow the lawn. Our mothers do not need a horse to go shopping. Young people do not need a horse to get to school.

4

But only a little more than a hundred years ago, all this was very different. Everywhere man wanted to go on land, he relied on the horse to get him there. And any belongings that he wanted to take with him had to be carried or pulled by horses.

Sometimes even travel by water required the help of the horse. If you have heard the old song about the Erie Canal, you know of one of the inland canals used to transport goods and passengers in the East. Boats and barges were pulled along these narrow waterways by horses waiting on the edges of the canals. In this way the horse supplied power on water as well as land.

Before we had engines and machines to help us, we needed the horse to get all kinds of work done. Man did not use the horse to have fun. Man needed the horse in order to live.

Let us suppose a man wanted to build a house. First, he needed a horse to help clear the land and drag away the rocks, trees and stumps. Then he used his horse to take logs to the mill to be sawed into planks. When the lumber was cut, the horse pulled it back home. He helped carry each beam and board until the house was built.

If the man wanted to plant crops on his land, he needed a horse to plow his fields and gather the harvest. If he lived in the South and owned a great plantation of cotton or tobacco, he needed a horse to carry him over the vast fields to inspect his crops. Or if he lived in the West and raised herds of cattle or sheep, he relied on horses to help tend his stock. He used the horse to round up his cattle and rope them, to herd them to better grazing lands and to take them to market in big cattle drives. He counted on the horse to guard the herd day and night. Even today horses are still used on ranches to help care for the cattle.

People who lived in cities needed the horse just as much as farmers and ranchers. Doctors visited their patients by horse and buggy. Successful merchants transported their goods in wagons pulled by long hitches of beautifully matched horses. When a gentleman courted his lady, he arrived in an elegant carriage drawn by a sleek, spirited pair of horses. If a fire broke out, the fire truck that rushed to the blaze was pulled by horse team. The mails were carried between big cities by horse-drawn coaches. Where there were no large cities, letters were transported by a horse and rider working for the Pony Express.

Bankers shipped gold and payroll money by speedy horse teams pulling specially guarded coaches. Even though bankers tried to protect their shipments, sometimes the money was stolen by bandits. The sheriff then used horses to chase the thieves. And the thieves, of course, used horses in their getaway!

It is only during the past hundred years that all these things have changed. If we look around us, we can see how many different kinds of machines man has had to invent to do jobs once performed by the faithful horse.

A hundred years may seem like a very long time indeed. But it really isn't so long when we think of the hundreds and hundreds of years before that when the horse alone served man's needs. In fact, scientists say that the horse was man's most important means of power for well over 6,000 years!

Today the horse no longer plays an important part in shaping events of the world. Yet, had it not been for the horse, it is hard to imagine what the world would be like today. That is why people in every land think of the horse with love and respect. So if it is true that the dog is "man's best friend," the horse is surely man's greatest partner.

Horses and wagons in the streets of New York City about 1870.

The Horse
Becomes a Horse

What if someone told you that you would not recognize a horse if you saw one? You would probably think that person was crazy. After all, everyone knows what a horse looks like.

For one thing, a horse is big—sometimes taller than a grown man. A horse *must* be big and strong to carry people on his back and pull heavy loads.

We also know that a horse has four long, slender legs, with which he can gallop at great speed. Naturally, at the bottom of his legs are his feet. But we know that the horse's feet are not like ours. Nor are his feet like the paws of a dog. The horse has no toes. Instead, his feet are nearly round and very, very hard. They are called hoofs. We can imagine how hard these hoofs are because of the sharp

The horse as we know him today. This is a painting of the race horse "Eclipse" by Edward Troye.

clippity-clop sound they make when the horse runs. We can remember the shape of the hoofs from the horseshoes we have seen. Horses wear these iron shoes to keep their hoofs in good condition.

Another thing we can see is that the horse has quite a long neck. He uses it to lean down to the ground to reach the hay and grass he eats. If we look at his head, we also notice that he has alert ears which poke up into the air. The horse can move his ears back and forth. But they always stick up firmly, never flopping down against his head like a dog's.

The horse's eyes are unusual, too. They are big and round and placed toward the sides of his face. They are not aimed directly ahead, like our own eyes, but slightly outward to the left and right. The horse can see ahead of him, behind and to the side all at once.

Just by listing the things we know about the horse, we can see how familiar he is to us. He is so familiar that it is hard to imagine being unable to recognize him. Yet the first horse who roamed the earth looked like no animal we know today. To meet him, we must first take a make-believe trip into the world as it was millions of years ago.

And what a strange land it was! The climate was warm and wet—even in places like Canada and Alaska. The land was not firm and dry, but a huge, steaming, oozing swamp. Warm mists lifted off the water and drifted into the thick, jungle-like overgrowth of plants, mosses and vines. Crashing through these steamy forests were all kinds of huge beasts, like the dinosaur, the brontosaur and the great tyrannosaur. After awhile, the dinosaurs began

Eohippus, the "dawn horse," was about as big as a small dog.

to die out. New varieties of animals appeared to take their place.

Not all of the new creatures were huge and frightening. One was quite the opposite. He was small, timid and furry—altogether a rather peaceful little fellow, we believe. He began living on earth about 60 million years ago, and scientists have named him *Eohippus. Eo* is the Greek word for dawn. *Hippos* is the Greek word for horse. So eohippus was the "dawn horse"—the first horse at the dawn of time.

If we look at eohippus we can see for ourselves

how different he was from the horse we know today.

First there is the matter of size. Eohippus was only about as large as a jack rabbit, or a small dog. He measured about twelve inches high from the top of his head to his toes. Because his legs were short, eohippus probably could not run very fast.

Stranger still, eohippus did not have hoofs like the horses we know. Each of his feet had toes. On the front feet were four toes. On the back feet were three toes.

Looking as he did, with a squat body and funny feet squishing through the mud, eohippus was a far cry from the speedy horses of today. And for this tiny primitive horse, life was a very dangerous business. There were beasts with long teeth to eat him and others with huge feet to trample him. Small wonder that eohippus spent most of his time scurrying away to find safety. He had to hide from his enemies because he had no means of defending himself.

The safest place for eohippus was the darkness of the forests. In the forests there were tender leaves for him to feed on with his tiny, sharp teeth. In the forests the leaves hung low enough for his short neck to reach. In the forests he could easily hide.

Eohippus survived this way for millions of years. But very gradually he began to change. Forty million years ago he was no longer the dawn horse. He was beginning to look different, so scientists have given him a different name. They call him the "middle horse" or *Mesohippus*.

One change was that mesohippus grew several inches taller than the dawn horse. His legs were longer, and he measured about as high as a sheep. Another change was that he had but three toes on each of his feet. Thanks to his longer legs and more streamlined feet, mesohippus could run a little faster and escape some of his enemies.

Mesohippus was also better equipped to sense danger. He had a bigger and much better brain than eohippus. His eyes were larger and rounder and placed near the sides of his face. This meant he could see to the side and the rear as well as ahead. He also grew bigger teeth and stronger jaws. With these he could browse on new kinds of plants and leaves.

Mesohippus scampered along this way until about 10 million years ago.

Over the course of millions of years, great changes had taken place on earth. There was movement in the earth's crust. Mountains formed, swamps dried up, forests thinned out. The earth became covered with vast, open plains.

With so few forests to hide in, the horse could no longer be a hiding creature. He had to find a new way to escape his enemies. He had to become a running creature.

Slowly his legs grew longer. Now he was the height of a pony. The toes at the sides of his feet became smaller so they barely touched the ground. The middle toe grew sturdy and large to give him swift, solid footing on the hard ground. Now he could run quite well.

Most important of all, the horse-creature learned to eat grass. Running was not completely strange to him. But grazing on the plains grass was very different from browsing on leaves. He had to grow

Mesohippus was the size of a sheep.

17

a longer neck in order to reach the grass. He had to develop large teeth and strong jaws to chew this new food. Now the new horse could do what no earlier relative had done. He could live by grazing on grass. That is why scientists call him *Merychippus,* the "first grazing horse."

If we look at merychippus we see an animal that looks a little like the horses we know today. Not a very pretty horse, but one we recognize as a distant relative. Only by looking closely at his feet will we see that there was one thing different about the first grazer. He still had toes. True, they were not very large toes. They did not even touch the ground. But they were there.

This difference disappeared about one million years ago. The horse became an animal with just a single large toe on each foot. This horse is known as *Pliohippus,* "more recent horse."

Once the horse lost his side toes, it was not long before he became big and swift and beautiful in all ways. He had alert eyes and ears to warn him of danger. He had long, powerful legs and firm hoofs to give him speed. He had a graceful neck and strong teeth and jaws so he could eat well. He lost the last traces of his primitive look. He became a mighty and splendid creature, a true horse. Scientists call him *Equus,* a Latin word that means simply "horse."

Merychippus, the first grazing horse. Notice the extra toes on his sturdy feet.

Pliohippus, the first one-toed horse.

Equus is the very horse we know today. He is the modern relative of little eohippus who lived 60 million years ago. He is the horse that finally survived the dangers and surprises of the forest, the plains, the wilderness.

Equus galloped wild and free until a new surprise entered his world. This surprise was a new creature on earth. A strange new creature called man.

The Horse Meets Man

Man and horse met for the first time many thousands of years ago. We do not know exactly where or when. But we do know that for a long, long time it seemed that they would never become friends.

The horse looked and lived just about the way he does today. But man was very different. Man was still a primitive creature. He did not know how to build houses for shelter. Instead, he lived among huge rocks, in caves and caverns. Caves were the best shelter man could find. Even so, they were not very comfortable. They were dark and cold. Man could not light or warm his cave-home because he did not know how to use fire.

The only way for man to keep warm was to

Early man depended on animals to survive. He used their meat for food and their skins for clothing.

bundle up in heavy clothing. But what clothing? Man did not know how to weave the fibers of wool or silk or cotton into cloth to protect his body. All he had to keep from freezing were the skins of animals, and these were what he wore.

Animals also provided man's food. Early humans liked vegetables as well as meat. But vegetables were only a small part of man's diet because he could only eat the plants he found growing wild. When he ate all these, his vegetable supply was gone. He did not know he could plant seeds and make his own garden. Nor did he have any tools for such farming.

Man did not have a hoe or a rake or a shovel or a plow. He did not have wheels or wagons. Without the wheel, he could not move heavy objects. He could not bring big, heavy things to his cave home. If he needed these things, he had to move himself to where they were. So he often moved from one cave-home to another. Early man had to be a wanderer.

He was a wanderer without a good home or fire or clothing or plentiful vegetables. He had to depend on animals to survive. He depended on their meat to keep him from starving and on their skins to keep him warm. So man was a hunter—and among the creatures he hunted was the horse.

Now we can understand why at first it appeared that man and horse could never become friends. When primitive man looked at the horse, all he saw was dinner and warm clothes. When the horse looked at man, all he saw was a dangerous killer. It was only natural that the horse would run in blind terror from this human hunter.

Early man had no idea that horses could be tamed

and made into friends. He had never seen anyone ride a horse. He had never seen a horse pull things. To man, the horse was simply another wild game animal. In fact, he seemed the perfect game animal for man's needs.

For one thing, the horse was so large that his flesh could supply several meals for a whole cave family. His hide was also large, providing the biggest, warmest robes and clothes. How much better it was, then, to kill one horse instead of half a dozen smaller animals.

Besides, the horse was easy for man to hunt. He was so tall that it was not difficult to see him. Most horses lived in herds which made them even easier to spot. Then, too, the horse was not dangerous.

These cave paintings were made by American Indians.

He would not attack the hunter. The worst that could happen was that the herd might escape by running away, for horses were quick to take fright.

Because horses were so timid and afraid, cave men were able to kill whole herds even without weapons. They could panic the horses into a stampede and drive them over steep drops. Then the cave people climbed down the cliffs to feast on their kill and gather the hides.

In this manner ancient man was able to kill hundreds of horses. At a primitive cave camp in France, skeletons have been found which show that over 100,000 horses were eaten there by early humans! At still another primitive settlement in France, a place called Lascaux, scientists have found

cave paintings which tell us more about the horse's importance to early man. Crude horse pictures cover much of the walls and ceilings of the cave. They are what we might call "wish" paintings. The cave men wished for real horses to come to their lands. They believed that by wishing very hard and making lots of horse paintings, real horses would soon be found.

These "wish" paintings did not really work any magic to help man. But it did not matter because, slowly but surely, man began discovering ways to help himself. He learned how to make weapons and crude tools. He learned how to use fire. He stumbled upon the important invention of the wheel. He discovered that he could plant seeds and farm little gardens of fruits and vegetables.

These discoveries came little by little, very gradually over many thousands of years. But each step led toward civilization. And each step led away from man's old way of surviving by killing the great horse herds.

With better weapons, for example, man became a more skillful hunter. He could bring down whatever game he wanted, so he did not have to pick on the easiest target. He did not need to slaughter a whole horse herd just for a couple of meals.

With fire he could keep his home warm. With tools to build things and wheels to carry them, he

Slowly, man learned to become a farmer as well as a hunter. Here, early men are using simple tools to plant seeds.

could improve his home and make it more comfortable. Man no longer had to be a wanderer. With his home a snug, safe living place, he did not need so many animal skins to keep warm. As he needed fewer hides, he again killed fewer horses.

By farming his little gardens, man was able to supply more vegetables for himself. So now he did not need to kill as many game animals to keep from starving.

Gradually man became a better and better farmer.

And gradually a new idea dawned on him. If he could raise his own plants at home, why couldn't he also raise his own animals? Instead of going out and killing his meat each day and having to eat it right away, he could capture live animals. He could bring these home to raise and care for, killing only as he needed fresh meat.

So man began keeping living creatures in pens near his home. Most of these creatures were small and harmless, quite safe for man to handle. Perhaps man caught young goats and sheep, or slow-moving oxen. They became tame and friendly. Man learned he could train the strong ones to pull things and use others to supply milk. In fact, after a while these primitive herds and flocks were no longer wild at all. They were the ancient relatives of our domestic animals—animals that lived at home with man.

But there was one animal man did not try to tame and keep. This was the horse. The horse was the last of all the major animals man learned to domesticate.

We cannot be sure exactly why this was so. Maybe man thought the horse was too big and strong and fast to be captured and made tame. Maybe, too, he saw no purpose in having a horse. He had other creatures for food. He had the plodding oxen to pull his burdens. And he still did not know that a horse could be ridden. So he did not try to catch living horses.

The only thing we *can* be absolutely sure of is that somewhere, sometime, something happened to change man's mind. We can guess that it probably started by accident. Perhaps it may have happened like this:

One day, while moving his flock of goats to a better pasture, a primitive farmer came upon a small, wild baby horse. It was wounded and bleeding. Its frightened mother had run away with the herd. The little horse's dark eyes were wide with fear as it watched the farmer come nearer. Its body trembled. Its slender legs struggled helplessly to bear it up and away.

The farmer felt sorry for the tiny creature. Though he was still a very primitive farmer, he had learned to love his own animals and care for their needs. He decided to bring it home and let his children look after it.

The children were excited to have a baby horse. They took good care of their new pet and soon its wounds healed. Soon, too, the little horse lost its fear of man. It grew to love its new family of human beings. Even when the horse grew big and strong, it remained gentle. It let the children climb on its back. It let them steer it here and there, stopping and starting, going fast or slow.

When the farmer saw his children riding the horse he decided he would try this new game, too. Cautiously he climbed on the horse's back. He started off slowly, until he saw how safe and gentle the animal was. Then he let the horse race faster and faster. It raced like the wild herds running on the plains. It raced like the wind that swept through the trees. Its feet drummed on the ground like mighty thunder, and the farmer's heart pounded in his chest.

Together they raced on, past a settlement of strangers who had never seen the farmer's tame horse. The strangers could not believe that a man was actually riding on a horse's back. They thought this must be some magical new creature that was half man and half horse! Terrified, they dropped their tools and weapons and ran for safety.

When the farmer returned home, his heart still pounded with excitement. Truly he had discovered something wondrous. He had found a means to move as fast as the wind. He had found a creature that could take him to far places and back in just a single day. With this creature he could go any-where he wanted. He could move his flocks to better pastures. He could use the horse's strength to pull things. Its power would make his clumsy wheels spin over the ground with a fierce speed.

But most of all, this creature made him feel strong

and mighty in his spirit. He had seen how the strangers had fled from the miracle of the horse and rider. His enemies, too, would run from his path. Never again would they enter his lands to kill and

A very old statue of a horse and rider.

steal what was his! Now he was truly safe and powerful.

From that moment on, the horse was as important to man as all his weapons and tools, as fire and the wheel and his garden. He knew that he must tell his friends of this great discovery so that never again would they kill a horse. From now on his people would love and protect this most marvelous of all creatures.

Horses of Dawn, Horses of Darkness

Many lucky "accidents," such as the one described in the last chapter, brought man and horse together in many parts of the world at the earliest dawn of civilization.

In one part of the world, however, man was especially quick to realize the importance of his new partner. This territory, at the eastern end of the Mediterranean Sea, stretched from Asia Minor southward to North Africa. This was the Middle East, in ancient times a land of mighty kingdoms.

Today much of the Middle East is parched, barren desert. But long ago, the country looked very different. Its plains were green and fertile. Lush grass grew thick, and an abundance of food could be harvested from the rich earth.

In Arabia, scientists have found rocks that bear unusual nicks and scars. These markings show that heavy rainfalls once drenched whole regions which are now desert sand. Between the Tigris and Euphrates Rivers lay the ancient kingdom of Mesopotamia, a land that long ago was warm, fertile and pleasant. It was a spot so perfect for man that some scholars believe Mesopotamia was the place the Bible calls the Garden of Eden.

Throughout much of the Middle East, the climate was warm and comfortable. Both people and horses could thrive without hardship. For man, life was no longer a bitter struggle simply to find food and shelter. He now had the tools and knowledge to raise what he needed to eat, to build a good shelter for his family, to make clothing from cloth. He was no longer a primitive creature. He was, in fact, beginning to have definite ideas about the way he should live. He was starting to formulate laws, religions and systems of government. All these things would help bring order to the new world man was creating.

Because people of early civilizations realized the value of horses, one of the very first laws they made was to forbid the eating of horseflesh. Even today one of the rules of the Orthodox Jewish faith forbids eating any creature which does not have cloven hoofs—hoofs with a split up the middle, like those

The Sumerian battle chariot was heavy and awkward, with its four solid-wood wheels. This one is being drawn by four donkeys.

of a cow or deer. This meant that animals of the horse family—horses, ponies, mules, donkeys—were spared from slaughter.

They were indeed more useful alive. Horses were used, for instance, in hauling materials to build houses. With chiseled stone or dried mud or brick, man found he could fashion a sturdy home of any size or shape he desired. He could build it in just the place he wished to live. Soon clusters of houses were being constructed in the most suitable places on the land. In time the clusters grew into whole cities.

As larger numbers of people gathered to live in these cities, new ways of life developed. Clearly, with so many people living close together, it no longer made sense for *all* of them to do *all* the chores involved in routine life. Why should a man continue being part farmer, part hunter, part house-builder, and so forth, when he was really best, perhaps, at making tools? All he need do now was specialize in making tools. He could then trade his tools for the other things he needed.

Thus man started to become a trader and businessman. The horse was vital to this new way of life. If a man was a tool-maker, he used a horse and cart to carry the metal and other raw materials he needed to his home. Later he delivered the finished tools by horse and cart.

Obviously man had come to rely on the horse as his best means of land transportation. Wherever he wished to travel, whatever far boundary he wished to explore, whether he wanted to transport himself or his trading goods, he counted on the horse to get the mission done swiftly.

It is impossible to number the many peaceful services the horse performed at the dawn of civilization. Unfortunately none was more important than his service in war. Here the horse was as dear to the warrior as life itself. Indeed, it was on the courage and skill of his horse that the soldier's very life depended.

As civilization expanded and rival kingdoms struggled to conquer each other, ever-increasing armies of horsemen surged through the Middle East. The land became an immense battlefield. Because the terrain was fairly level, it was well suited to the clash of horse troops. In these open plains there was room to maneuver and to charge at full speed. Horsemen could dart at the enemy, dodge away, return again to the skirmish, then suddenly retreat at a gallop to safety.

The use of horses in battle was at first very different from the kind of calvary charges we see in Western movies. It was not, for example, the custom for early warriors to ride astride the horse's back. This was not because people didn't know how to ride. It was because they felt they could fight better from a standing position in special lightweight battle-carts known as chariots.

Among the oldest types of chariots were those used by a people called the Sumerians. There were two models, one with two wheels and one with four. The four-wheeled cart was not much fancier than an ordinary wagon. The wheels were circular slabs of solid wood, which made the chariot heavy and difficult to control. Worse still, the Sumerians relied

The Greek chariot with spoked wheels was light and fast.

on wild asses instead of horses to pull these vehicles. With a donkey-like creature as a war steed and a rickety wagon as a chariot, it is hard to imagine the Sumerian horse trooper as a very fearful enemy!

Improvement was clearly in order and it was the Assyrians who took the next step forward. While they continued to use the old-fashioned chariot with four solid-wood wheels, they took to using horses to supply the pulling power. Soon this led to still further progress. Suddenly in widely scattered nations throughout the region a discovery was made that had a great effect on chariot warfare. This discovery was the spoked wheel.

Spoked wheels came into use in Asia Minor by the war-like Hittites and their neighbors the Mitanni. Farther south in Egypt and Babylonia they were also adopted. The new type of wheel made the chariots light and easy to control. Now the forces of Egypt, with their two-man chariot, and the Hittites, who used a three-man chariot, could swiftly speed across the plains in search of further conquests.

Later still it became popular to employ mounted cavalry as well as charioteers. Among certain nations, the riding skill of the warriors was altogether astounding. The horse soldiers of Parthia, for example, invented a trick maneuver to outwit their enemies. The mounted Parthian warrior, with bow and arrow raised to shoot, charged full speed right on past the enemy, as though unable to control his horse. The enemy was thus fooled into thinking he was safe. But suddenly the Parthian whirled about-face on top of his horse. Now, riding backwards at a gallop, he released the deadly arrow, catching the enemy completely off guard.

This athletic skill was a traditional mark of warriors dating from earliest history through the time of the mighty Roman Empire. The soldiers of the Middle East and the growing civilizations around the Mediterranean Sea were proud of their bodies. They did not wear a great deal of armor. Instead, they relied on skill and control of their strength to bring them glory in battle.

The horses used by these warriors were ideal for such athletic fighting. Though they were fairly small, light in build and slender through the legs, they were extremely sturdy. They were also amazingly fleet and could run long distances without tiring. Because they were compact in size, they did not require a great deal of food and so could survive well in battle when food and water were in short supply.

Very much like their riders, the Eastern horses were agile and nimble-footed. They were creatures of fiery spirit with nostrils that flared wide and pink in the excitement of battle. It is because of this fiery spirit that horses of Eastern breeding are referred to as "hot-blooded" horses.

Today's Arabian horse is the descendent of this hot-blooded strain. He is the oldest breed we know, the very horse used by ancient Eastern conquerors.

The Arabian horse and his relatives were the first horses to be put to use by civilized man. But, as we know, they were far from the last.

In the fourth century A.D., the mighty Roman Empire collapsed. The countries of Europe, once kept in order by the Romans, now entered a new period of history—a period called the Dark Ages. The glimmer of civilization, which had spread to Europe from the Middle East and the Mediterranean, suddenly fell beneath a cloud. Europe came under attack by barbarian invaders—crude, savage tribes that roamed the continent.

The horses used by the barbarians were far dif-

Today's Arabian horse is a close relative of the horses used by ancient warriors of the Middle East.

ferent from the light, nimble mounts of the Middle East. But they were very well suited to the strategy of the barbarian fighters and to the rugged, mountainous terrain of Europe.

Unlike the warriors of the East and Mediterranean, the barbarians did not rely on skillful training and athletic grace in battle. Instead, they carried lots of heavy wooden weapons. They wore thick padding to protect their bodies. They rode on huge, awkward lumbering horses native to northern Europe. These slow, plain-looking animals were called "cold-blooded" horses because their temperament was cool and sluggish compared to the fiery Eastern horses.

The roving invaders of the Dark Ages, mounted on their enormous steeds, fought with the strategy of a modern tank troop. They simply mowed down anything in their way. This may not sound like a very noble and glamorous way of fighting. Yet these tribes were the forerunners of the most glamorous horsemen in all history—the knights of chivalry in their shining armor.

Gradually, with the passage of many centuries, the tribal warriors of Europe began settling into more civilized ways. They built magnificent castles in which to live. They fortified themselves with walls and moats as defense against attackers. In command of the castle was a noble lord or prince who was served by the knights and squires of his domain.

Naturally, the lords and knights sought to improve their battle tools. Soon they developed a wide variety of weapons made of metal. To protect their bodies

Often, both a knight and his charger wore a full suit of armor when they rode into battle.

they wore armor made of chain mesh—small metal links woven together and sewn to padding. Later they improved this armor by attaching solid metal plates to the mesh links. Finally, they abandoned the mesh altogether in favor of a suit of solid plate-metal armor which covered the wearer from head to toe.

Now these knights were truly glorious to behold as they rode forth to battle. Dressed in glimmering steel with colorful plumes on the crest of their helmets, they followed the fluttering banners at the head of their legions. No longer were they primitive savages plundering the land. They were men of honor whose duty was to defend their lord and master. And no longer did they ride clumsy horses of the forest wilderness. Now they were mounted on handsome chargers, bred to size and power, horses able to carry a knight plus 200 pounds of armor through the day's battle.

These war horses were still of cold-blooded strains. But over the years, as man bred them for the service of his wars, they developed a proud, impressive bearing that gave them a special kind of dignity. Like the Ugly Duckling, the heavy charger grew to be a creature of strange, majestic beauty. And, like the sword, the shield and the coat of arms, the charger became a symbol of the gallant age of knights and troubadours.

The Horse
in the New World

In 1492 Christopher Columbus sailed across the Atlantic Ocean and discovered the New World. It was a world that, strangely enough, was completely barren of horses.

We do not know exactly why this was so. We know that in prehistoric times eohippus and his relatives lived in North America. Preserved horse skeletons, called fossils, have been found in many parts of the American West. These show that prehistoric horses existed in our country until about ten thousand years ago. Then, mysteriously, they all disappeared. Perhaps they were killed by some disease, or by a change in climate that destroyed the grass and plants. No one really knows what happened. All we know is that when the first explorers came, not a horse was to be found in America.

The Spanish explorer Hernan Cortés brought the first horses back to America. The sight of men on horseback was so strange to the natives of the New World that even the bravest Indians were struck with terror when they saw them. Thus the Spanish adventurers had a strong advantage. Most Indians were simply too frightened of the horses to put up much of a fight against the invaders.

But in time the Indians grew wiser and took to stealing or trading for Spanish horses. They raised horses of their own and learned to ride them with great skill. The horses rapidly multiplied and soon wild herds roamed over the countryside. In the West many of these wild horses, called mustangs, continued to run free for many years.

In the East, however, most of the horses were recaptured. Some were sold by friendly Indians to the settlers arriving from many countries in Europe to seek their fortune in the New World.

At first the settlers' fortune was nothing but hardship. They were faced with a vast, uncivilized land inhabited only by primitive tribes. The tasks ahead were enormous, and so was the need for horses to help them. There were fields to be cleared of trees and rocks and stubborn stumps. The untouched soil had to be tilled and planted. The harvest had to be reaped and gathered. Timber had to be felled

Indians used horses and dogs to carry their belongings when they moved from camp to camp.

and hewn by hand into beams and boards to build homes. Supplies had to be hauled from tiny villages to the new settlements in the wilderness.

There was no end to the things which had to be done—and no end to the jobs a single horse had to be able to handle to help his colonial master. The old heavy charger of Europe was simply too large and cumbersome to be the all-purpose animal required by the Atlantic settlers. Just feeding such a gigantic creature was more than most settlers could afford. As for the nimble horses of the ancient East, they were far away and costly to buy.

Fortunately, however, the wild descendents of the Spanish horses had many qualities of the horses of the Middle East. This was because centuries earlier the Spanish had mated large numbers of Eastern hot-blooded horses with the huge cold-blooded horses of Europe. The result was a type of horse with the best features of both—the strength of the powerful charger combined with the endurance, speed and handsome looks of the Middle-Eastern strain.

These cross-bred horses traveled with the Spanish to the New World. They were the very stock the settlers used to develop the all-purpose horse they needed—a new breed which would work with the pioneers to forge a home out of the wilderness. In colonial times, this breed had a very fancy name. It was called the Famous and Celebrated Colonial Quarter Pather. Later it became known simply as the Quarter Horse. Of course, later settlers brought other kinds of horses to America from Europe, but this was the first breed to be raised in the New World, and today it is the most popular horse in the nation.

The Quarter Horse was especially popular in the mid-Atlantic colonies such as Maryland and Virginia and places farther south. It was perfectly suited to the demands of colonial life. Like its Middle Eastern relatives, it was rather small and did not require much food to keep in good condition. It was also rugged, powerful and sturdy, able to work all day without becoming tired. And it was quick and cat-like on its feet. A Quarter Horse could sprint to a start like a bolt of lightning and stop on a dime in the midst of a full gallop.

With so many talents, there was practically no job a colonial Quarter Horse couldn't tackle. They were used as work horses to clear the fields and till the farmland. They were used as cow ponies to drive the settlers' small herds into their barnyard cow pens. They served as cart-horses, drawing wagon-loads of lumber and trading goods from house to house and village to village. On Sundays, they might be seen hitched to buggies, taking the family to church. Or the master of the house might saddle up and ride to town to catch up on the local news.

In addition, the Quarter Horse was often the settlers' chief source of pleasure and excitement. Most of the early settlers were poor, hard-working people with little time or money to spend on fun and gaiety. But rich or poor, almost everyone owned a horse. And all it took was two good runners to put everyone in the mood for a lively test of speed.

Thus, racing became a favorite pastime among the Atlantic colonies. A whole town would turn out on holidays to watch the horses compete, and often the crowd was as frisky as the racers. Spectators

Quarter Horses rounding up a herd of cattle.

argued over which horse was faster and cheered loudly for their favorites. Tradesmen hawked their goods, gamblers placed their bets and children jumped up and down excitedly at the finish line.

The race itself was much different from the horse racing we know today. In the first place, it was not run on a large oval track. People didn't have time to clear a whole mile of land for a sporting event. There was too much other work to be done, just in order to survive. Instead, the race was usually run down the main street of the town. Sometimes, if the town was not big enough to have a street, a short racing path was hacked through the woods.

The distance was usually eighty rods—about a quarter of a mile.

Another difference was that in each race only two horses competed against each other. Today any number of horses may run in a contest. The colonial system was called "match racing" because one horse was matched against the other.

The race was actually "started from scratch." The starting point was a line scratched in the dirt road with a stick. And the horses began running "at the drop of a hat," for the customary starting signal was the tossing of a hat in the air. When the hat hit the ground, the race was underway. We use these expressions even today, but few people realize that they originated hundreds of years ago at colonial horse races.

In these early races, the Quarter Horse really shone. His whirlwind speed over short distances sent him shooting over the finish line when his clumsier rivals had barely gotten started. He was so superior at the quarter-mile distance that this is how he earned the name Quarter Horse.

Dazzling though he was as a racing performer, there was still another feature about the Quarter Horse that was equally important to the settlers. This feature was his gentle, intelligent nature.

From dawn to dusk the Quarter Horse worked side by side with his master and other members of the family. He shared so much of the settlers' everyday life that he became as friendly as a children's pet. He seemed to like the company of man. In helping his master look after the livestock, he also developed a particular liking for other animals around the farm.

The Quarter Horse's unusual interest in other animals proved to be a valuable asset to the pioneers who pushed westward. As the great cattle ranches of the West began to flourish, the special know-how or "cow savvy" of the Quarter Horse made him perfect for handling the huge herds. In the dust of the great cattle drives, by the branding fires at

The Morgan was the all-purpose horse of the New England colonists.

round-up time, or sprinting after a stray calf, it was always the Quarter Horse who proved to be the cowboy's finest helper.

In the meantime, up north in the New England colonies, another hardy breed of all-purpose horse was developing. The northern version of the Quarter Horse was a breed called the Morgan, in honor of the stallion named Justin Morgan who established the strain.

Among the many things Morgans had in common with Quarter Horses was their size. They were relatively small and chunky but similarly powerful, steadfast workers. Like the Quarter Horse, Morgans

As roads were built, more and more people traveled by carriage rather than on horseback.

could work long hours without tiring and handle any variety of jobs. Here again, the horse helped his master with the routine chores of farm work. At planting time he pulled the plow. At harvest time he drew the reaper, and hauled wagons to gather the yield. If there were errands to be done in town, he could take his owner by carriage or carry his rider astride, for Morgans were pleasant riding

horses. Like the Quarter Horse, they were often raced under saddle over the traditional quarter-mile distance. But the greatest of all his assets was yet to be discovered.

As the New England countryside became more settled, roads were cleared for travel between towns and villages. More of the colonists began to travel in the comfort of a carriage or buggy instead of on horseback. People traveling by carriage did not wish to bounce over the rocks and ruts of these rough dirt roads at a full gallop, however. They required what was known as roadsters—fast horses who could cover the roads at a steady, strong, trotting gait.

It was discovered that the Morgan strain produced not only good sprinters but also fine roadsters, able to pull colonial carriages with amazing ease and speed. Morgans became the most popular of all roadster types and their swift trot ruled the early byways of New England. Soon, in fact, the proud colonists who owned Morgans couldn't resist racing one another along their route. This gave rise to a new kind of racing the world had never known before—the trotting race.

Thus, like the Quarter Horse who went west to open up the frontier, the Morgans earned a place of honor in the story of colonial days. They provided the chief means of travel linking New England's early communities. In addition, they founded a new type of racing that would spread to many parts of the world. They helped to establish the young nation as a country of fine sportsmen and matchless horses.

Horses Make
the Country Thrive

The early colonial horses did their job well. America in the 1800's was no longer a rugged colonial outpost. It was an independent nation, strong and prosperous. In the East, trade and industry were growing rapidly, bringing wealth to successful merchants and factory owners. In the South, great plantations of tobacco and cotton stretched as far as the eye could see, earning riches for southern land-owners. The Midwest was no longer a lonely wilderness, but a region of fertile, productive farms— a vast "wheat belt" that would feed the nation. In the West were the mines, timber and countless herds of beef and sheep that turned the frontier into a land of flourishing ranches and settlements.

The young nation was indeed a land of opportunity. But only with the help of the horse could opportunity be turned into success. People quickly realized that they needed not only more horses and better horses, but different kinds of horses.

As the country continued its rapid growth, progress created special jobs. Somehow man would have to find or breed horses with the special qualities to fit these jobs. The all-purpose horse, once so vital to the colonists, would now be replaced by a whole variety of horse "specialists."

As we have already mentioned, the Quarter Horse discovered his new specialty out on the Western range. His natural feeling for other animals suited him perfectly to cattle work. His agility and great sprinting speed combined with his toughness made him a brilliant performer in his new career as a cow pony. The prosperity of the West depended largely on cattle—and caring for cattle depended largely on the Quarter Horse.

Now farmers began to look for horses that were "specialists" in farm work. The 1800's was a time of immense agricultural growth. The Midwest, pioneered by men like Daniel Boone, was no longer frontier territory. The land was settled. Tilled earth and growing crops reached on for miles without end. The landscape looked like a giant puzzle with large, rectangular pieces—squared-off fields of rich brown soil, tawny wheat, and lush green corn

In the mid-1800's, the farmland of the Midwest was a checker-board of planted fields.

stalks. Here would be a major source of the new nation's bread.

To plant and harvest these miles of crops, farmers needed horses of tremendous size and power, with huge shoulders to shove against the harness and muscular haunches to thrust against the ground. Only horses of great brute strength could strain into the collar hour after hour, day after day. Sometimes they would work knee-deep in mud. Sometimes the ground would be as hard as cement. But still they must haul the heavy farm equipment, plowing the mud and crusted earth into neat furrows for planting.

Farmers were not the only people facing the need for horses of extraordinary pulling power. Successful merchants in bustling cities used heavy wagons loaded to the brim with goods and supplies. No ordinary horse or team of two could haul this kind of weight. Four or five trips to the same place would be required to make the deliveries, thus slowing down trade. Somehow stronger horses had to be found if business was to continue thriving.

To acquire such horses, America turned to Europe. In Belgium, France, and particularly England, strains of giant horses were already proving to be excellent workers on the farm. Their great power made them equally suitable for the city merchant's shipping and hauling.

These heavy horses were generally referred to as work horses, plow horses or draft horses. They were a cold-blooded type whose towering size traced directly to the war horses of the Dark Ages. Strange as it may seem, the mud-spattered plow horse, huge and humble, and the city draft horse, clip-clopping over cobblestone streets, were descendents of the great chargers gloriously ridden into battle by knights of chivalry.

When guns and cannon were introduced as weapons of war, their proud military service had come to an end. Armor became useless and soon was abandoned—and with it the massive chargers once

The Belgian horse, the heaviest of the working breeds.

needed to carry the weight of armed warriors. But the farmers of Europe had discovered that the ex-war horse could be harnessed up to plow the fields. He could, in fact, do twice the work of any other horse. Soon horsemen and farmers began taking special care to breed only the finest strains of work horses. These were the breeds imported by America to do the heavy labor on the country's farms and roads.

From Belgium came the heaviest of these breeds. Known simply as the Belgian horse, this chestnut-colored animal has a wide, thick-bodied appearance and weighs well over a ton.

From France came the Percheron, named for *La Perche,* the northwestern section of France where the breed was developed. Percherons are usually black or gray in color and are noted for their handsome looks as well as their strength.

From England came both the tallest and the smallest members of the group. The Shire, over a foot taller than ordinary horses, is distinguished by the growth of silky hair around his feet. Among breeders this hair is known as a horse's "feathers." More compact in size is the Suffolk Punch, a willing worker whose trimmer build and smaller appetite made him a thrifty horse for the farmer of modest means.

From Scotland came the Clydesdale, another

Percherons are often used today as circus performers.

feather-legged breed. The Clydesdale's flashy looks and spirited step made him a favorite of city merchants who wanted horses that looked sleek and snappy.

Farmers and merchants thus filled their needs with horses imported from abroad. But there were no such ready-made breeds to meet the quite different demands arising in the South. This was a region where cotton and tobacco brought great wealth to plantation owners. These crops, and others as well, were grown on tracts of land so vast that even their owners were not always sure exactly where their properties ended. A planter could ride from dawn till dusk without reaching the limits of his land. Such rides were often necessary, for it was important that he inspect his crops and direct the daily farm work.

Long hours spent in the saddle were far from enjoyable if the horse moved with a rough gait. Speed was not important since the planter wanted to take his time, pausing to give orders and look things over carefully. The essential need was comfort—a horse that moved so smoothly and pleasantly that a full day of riding would not be tiring.

Naturally such a horse had to have plenty of endurance to manage many miles of steady travel. Then, too, successful planters were men of pride and dignity. Their horses had to be eye-catching prancers fit to dazzle the neighbors and townsfolk.

For such needs southern horsemen developed two breeds. Out of Kentucky came what was originally called the Kentucky Saddle Horse—a sleek high-stepping dandy with neck and tail held in handsome arch. Now known as the American Saddle Horse, he is famed for his easy, rocking gaits. Indeed some Saddle Horses can move at specially taught gaits so smooth and gliding that the horse scarcely seems to be moving at all.

A high-stepping American Saddle Horse.

From Tennessee came a breed called the Tennessee Walking Horse. The Walking Horse, too, is a dazzling high-stepper. But he is famed most of all for his swift, running walk, as gentle on the rider as the sway of an old rocking chair.

Once again man was able to mold the horse to suit his wishes. And once again the horse was able to serve an important purpose in man's work.

Speed was of no importance on the peaceful plantations of the old South. But around large cities life moved at a faster pace. New roads were cleared and old roads were improved to permit swifter travel. But coaches and carriages could only move as fast as the Morgans and other roadsters trotting out in front. If real advances were to be made, they had to begin with the horse.

Efforts to increase the speed of roadsters resulted in another valuable breed. This new roadster was called the Standardbred—so named because these horses had to trot a mile within a special time limit or standard in order to qualify for racing.

Developed to serve as a roadster and as a harness racer, the Standardbred was such a success that all other rivals were left in the dust. His low, long-reaching strides devoured the ground while behind him, spinning faster and faster, were the wheels that kept America on the move.

Each of the breeds we have discussed earned his

Standardbred trotters on Harlem Lane in New York City in 1870.

measure of man's respect through hard, honest work. Oddly enough, however, the horse admired most of all was a breed never intended for work of any kind. His fame was based on his brilliance as an athlete, a star performer in the world of sport. He was a luxury horse whose fantastic speed and

long-distance endurance revolutionized the nature of racing.

This mighty horse was the Thoroughbred. His history begins in England in about 1700, when three stallions from the Middle East were bred to native English mares. Descended from the Eastern stallions were three more stallions named Eclipse, Matchem and Herod. The amazing speed of this second three, and the speed they passed on to their children, established them as the founding fathers of the Thoroughbred—the fastest horse in the entire world.

Thoroughbreds were imported into America and took command of the racing scene. By now there was enough land cleared to build large oval tracks for horse racing. Races of greater distance, suited to the Thoroughbred's great stamina, soared to popularity, and the old-style Quarter Horse sprints disappeared from the East altogether.

The stunning speed and driving courage of the Thoroughbred racer quickly brought new luster to a sport as old as the friendship between men and horses. The fate of working horses would one day be threatened by progress and machinery. But the sporting Thoroughbred would endure forever simply to serve man's pleasure.

Horses Today

In the 1800's the energy of the horse was a basic tool to progress. But in the 1900's inventions devised by man's own mind began a whole new rush of advancement.

Steel tracks tunneled through mountains and across the wide floor of the deserts. The huff and roar of the steam engine, nicknamed the "iron horse," linked the country from coast to coast. Trains quickly became the fundamental means of travel and of shipping goods to territories far away.

On the nation's roads, there sputtered another new invention. This was the automobile—the so-called "horseless carriage" powered by a gasoline engine measured in "horsepower." Almost overnight it spelled the end of the Standardbred and other roadsters used for private carriages.

Soon the gasoline engine was used not only to power automobiles, but plows and mowers, reapers, tractors, trucks—all sorts of heavy machinery. And this machinery began to replace the work horse on the nation's farms and in the cities. Thus, even before the airplane began to speed passengers through the skies, the horse had come to the end of his days as man's most efficient means of land transportation.

With practically all his jobs now taken away, it looked for a long time as if the horse would become a forgotten creature. But an unexpected twist of fate was to bring him quite a different future.

Once, except for the rich, people had to devote every waking moment to earning a living. But now, especially in America, hundreds of thousands of working men and women had enough money to live in comfort and more time than ever before to enjoy leisure activities—thanks to the efficiency of the machines which had replaced the horse. They could enjoy sports and hobbies and do-it-yourself projects. They could rediscover the horse as a friend with whom to share spirited fun and relaxation. And this they have done in every part of the country.

A century ago Thoroughbred racers gave the first faint hint that the horse could find favor with man simply by filling a need for pleasure. But no one dreamed then that this was what was to come—and

Thoroughbreds are the fastest horses in the world.

not for Thoroughbreds alone, but for horses of every background and bloodline.

The speedy Thoroughbred is still king in racing. Star athletes of the track, such as Nashua, Swaps, Native Dancer, Buckpasser and Kelso, the mightiest of them all, have brought the thrill of the "sport of kings" to a growing throng of racing fans, rich and poor, young and old. It doesn't matter how many or how few races a person has seen—there is something unforgettable about the roar of hoofs thundering toward the finish line, and the courage of a racer whose every stride toward the wire seems to say: "No matter what, I won't give up."

Because they are excellent jumpers as well as the swiftest runners, Thoroughbred horses are also used for hunting by children and adults all over the country. With baying foxhounds to follow the scent, riders set out on fall mornings to chase the pesky fox, an age-old threat to the farmer's crops and chickens. Across the meadows and over fences they gallop, as the brassy toot of hunting horns fills the air.

The Thoroughbred's jumping ability has also made him the center of attraction in the jumping events in horse show competition. The crowd is held spellbound as the tall, lean Thoroughbred soars with effortless ease over hurdles the height of seven feet and more.

In the spotlight of the show ring, the working breeds have found new fame as well. The American Saddle Horse and the Tennesee Walking Horse, once the pride of the South's plantations, prance around the ring as if they alone commanded the universe. The audience goes wild with applause as these gleaming steppers glide through their special gaits.

One would never guess that the calmer relatives of these sleek, strutting Saddle Horses and Walkers are so gentle, as well as comfortable, that they are the favorite mounts of many inexperienced riders. They are the perfect horse for a sunny afternoon of peaceful wandering through field and woodland just for relaxation.

Morgans and Arabians are other breeds which have earned a faithful following among horselovers who ride for pleasure. The sturdy, versatile little Morgan is so friendly he can be ridden by anyone and so willing that he can do just about anything. Under saddle, the Morgan has proved a consistent winner on special trail rides of a hundred miles or even more. These contests are designed to test a horse's stamina. Morgans have shown that they can withstand the hardships of long-distance travel better than any other breed except the Arabian, who also excels in this special event.

In harness the Morgan has all the fancy footwork to make him an appealing carriage horse. Yet his nature is so sweet that children can climb all over him and ask him to pull them on their skis or draw an old-fashioned sleigh in winter. In horse shows the Morgan displays the full range of his gifts by appearing in harness classes, riding classes and even in heavy horse events, testing how much weight he can drag in case he were needed once again to help with farm work.

The Arabian continues to win acclaim for his dazzling beauty as well as his stunning long-distance endurance triumphs. One Arabian horse, at the ripe age of 22, set a cross-country record by traveling from

Oregon to New Hampshire in 21 days. His average speed was 119 miles per day!

A highlight of many horse shows is a special class in which Arabian horses and their riders appear in the native costume and equipment of desert Bedouin tribes.

The Standardbred horse, king of the roads until the invention of the automobile, has also managed to survive by bringing excitement to man's leisure hours. In recent years harness racing has become a favorite competitive sport among people who live in the country, where some of its friendly, old-fashioned atmosphere is still preserved. For those who live near metropolitan areas, Standardbred trotting is a popular nighttime entertainment.

Even the hulking work-horse breeds, whose towering strength did so much to build the nation's farms and commerce, still have their place in man's leisure activities. At country fairs and expositions, teams compete in strenuous weight-pulling events. The mood is tense as pound after pound is added to the load. One by one the teams are eliminated if they fail to move the burden, until just a single team is left that can prove it is up to the task.

Handsome Percherons are found in the circus, answering the signals of bareback riders who leap and twirl on their broad, gray backs. Hitches of powerful draft horses, in America the Budweiser

These powerful work horses are competing in a weight-pulling contest at the Iowa State Fair.

Clydesdales, and in England the Whitbread Shires, are in demand for parades and exhibitions.

For plain dirt-flying, hair-raising fun, there is nothing quite like the rodeo. Here the trusty Quarter Horse stars in such contests as steer wrestling and calf roping. With his time-tested knack for judging other animals, the Quarter Horse places himself in perfect position so the steer-wrestling

Cowboy and horse work as a team in the steer-wrestling contest.

cowboy can leap to the horns of the steer and twist its neck until it falls to the ground. The cowboy who grounds his steer in the fastest time wins the contest.

Similarly, in the calf-roping event, the Quarter

Horse trails the escaping calf at exactly the right distance so the cowboy's rope can find its mark. Then the horse skids to a stop. As the cowboy rushes to tie the legs of his calf, the horse continues to help by constantly backing away and keeping the rope firm and taut. Thus, the calf cannot scramble away before the fast-working roper has tied him up, hopefully in winning time.

A Lippizaner.

The best horse of all is the family pet. This girl is teaching her pony some tricks.

Quite opposite from the reckless world of the rodeo are the controlled, graceful maneuvers of the famous White Horses of Vienna—the Lippizaners. The pirouettes, the lordly leaps, the turns in mid-air performed by these horses are as precise as the movements of ballet dancers.

Despite his beauty and dazzling performance, it is not the glamorous Lippizaner who is the most important horse today. Nor is it the mighty Thoroughbred or the plucky Quarter Horse or even the graceful, courageous Arabian.

The horse that ranks highest may be of no particular breed at all, with a pedigree as scrambled as breakfast eggs. He may come in just about any color, size or shape. He is the family pet who lives in his owner's back yard, or in a neighbor's barn or at the local boarding stable.

He is the horse who comes to greet you at the pasture fence. He is the friend who shares your high spirits on a brisk ride through crimson autumn leaves. He listens when you talk to him, and stands with good-natured patience when you haul a friend aboard so that two can ride double on his back. He is more than the perfect pet, he is truly a comrade and friend. He offers affection as enduring as his age-old service to man. In his own way, he is a champion worth more than any prizewinner in the world.

Index

in Middle East, 33–40
uses today, 3, 70–79
Horse racing, 49–52, 56, 68, 71, 74
Horse show, 3, 72
Hot-blooded horses, 40–48
Hunting, 3, 72

I
Indians, 46

J
Jumping, 3, 72

K
Kentucky Saddle Horse, *see* American Saddle Horse
Knights, 42–44

L
Lascaux, 25
Lippizaner, 79

M
Merychippus, 17
Mesohippus, 16
Morgan, Justin, 53

Morgan, 53–56, 65, 73

P
Percheron, 61, 74
Pliohippus, 18
Plow horses, *see* Work horses

Q
Quarter Horse, 48–53, 58, 75–77

R
Riding, 3, 72–73, 79
Rodeo, 3, 75

S
Shire, 62, 75
Standardbred, 65, 67, 74
Suffolk Punch, 62

T
Tennessee Walking Horse, 65, 72
Trotters, 56, 65, 74
Thoroughbred, 67–68, 70–72

W
War horses, 36–44, 60
Work horses, 60–63, 68, 70, 74

About the Author

PAT JOHNSON began riding at the age of three, and has been working with horses or writing about them practically ever since. At the age of seven, she began showing horses and later, while still in school, taught riding and worked on a breeding farm.

After college, Miss Johnson worked in the editorial department of *Sports Illustrated*, and as an editor at Gold Medal Books. She now lives in Greenwich, Connecticut, where she devotes her time to free-lance writing. She is the author of books about horses for both children and adults, including *Horse Farm, Horse Fever*, and *The Treasury of Horses*.

About the Illustrator

WALTER D. OSBORNE is a leading photographer of horses, whose work has been shown in exhibitions and museum collections. His photographs have been used to illustrate many books, including *Marguerite Henry's All About Horses*, and *The Treasury of Horses*. A writer as well as a photographer, Mr. Osborne co-authored *The Treasury of Horses* with Miss Johnson, and has written two other books on his own, *The Quarter Horse* and *Horse Racing*. Mr. Osborne now lives in St. Michaels, Maryland.